Written by Fariha

Illustrated by Fariha

Dedicated for my baby, Isa

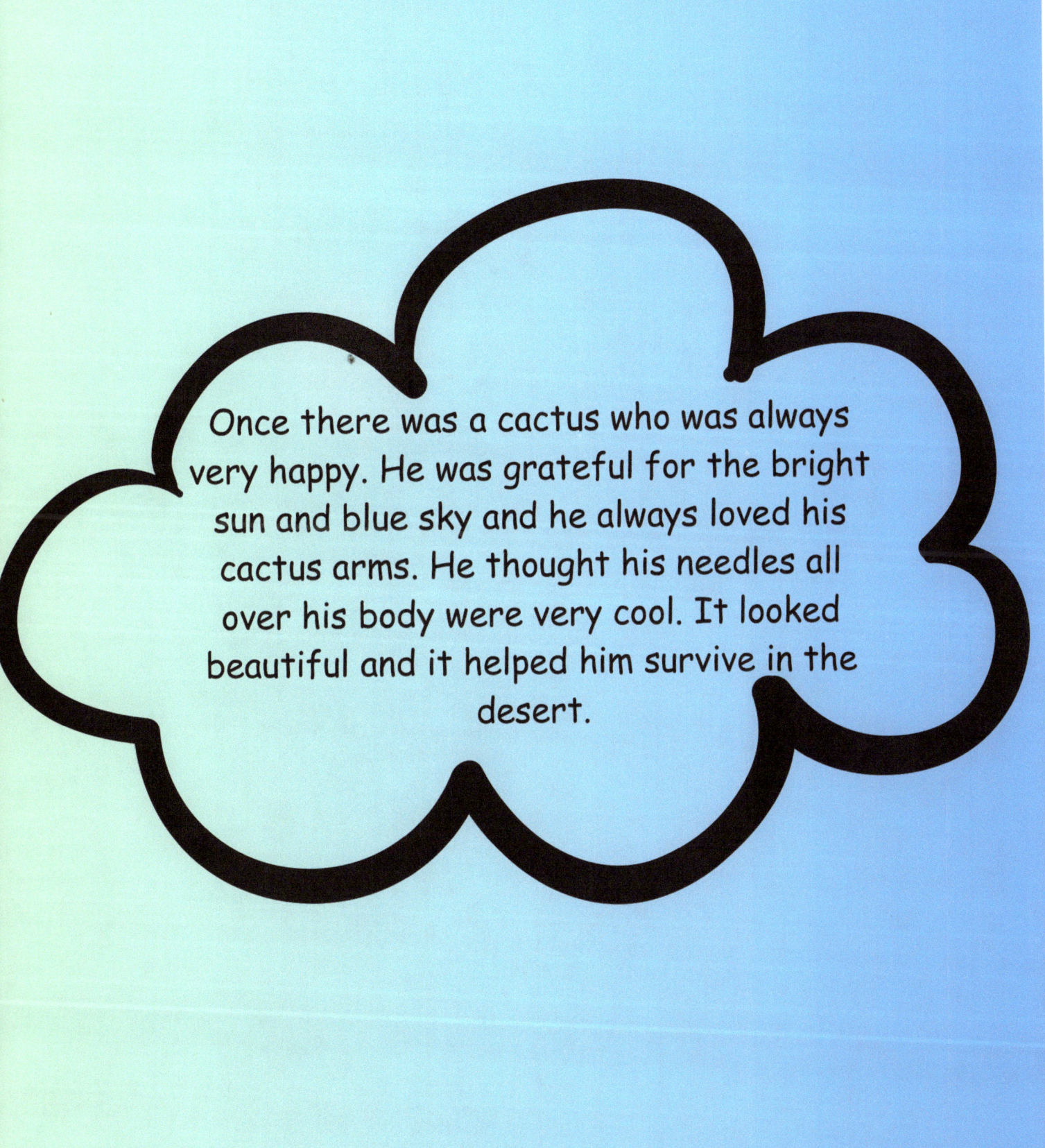

Once there was a cactus who was always very happy. He was grateful for the bright sun and blue sky and he always loved his cactus arms. He thought his needles all over his body were very cool. It looked beautiful and it helped him survive in the desert.

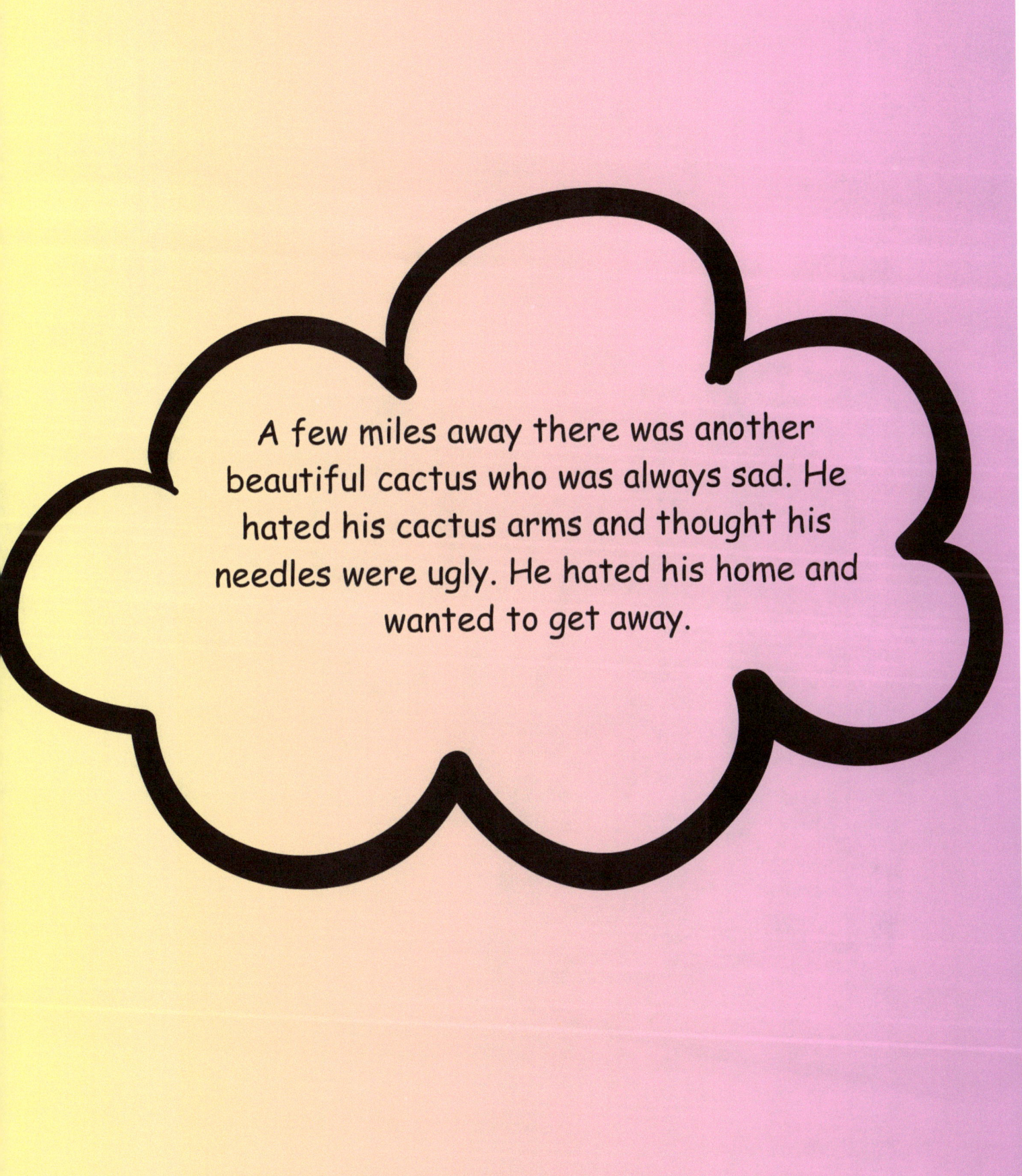

A few miles away there was another beautiful cactus who was always sad. He hated his cactus arms and thought his needles were ugly. He hated his home and wanted to get away.

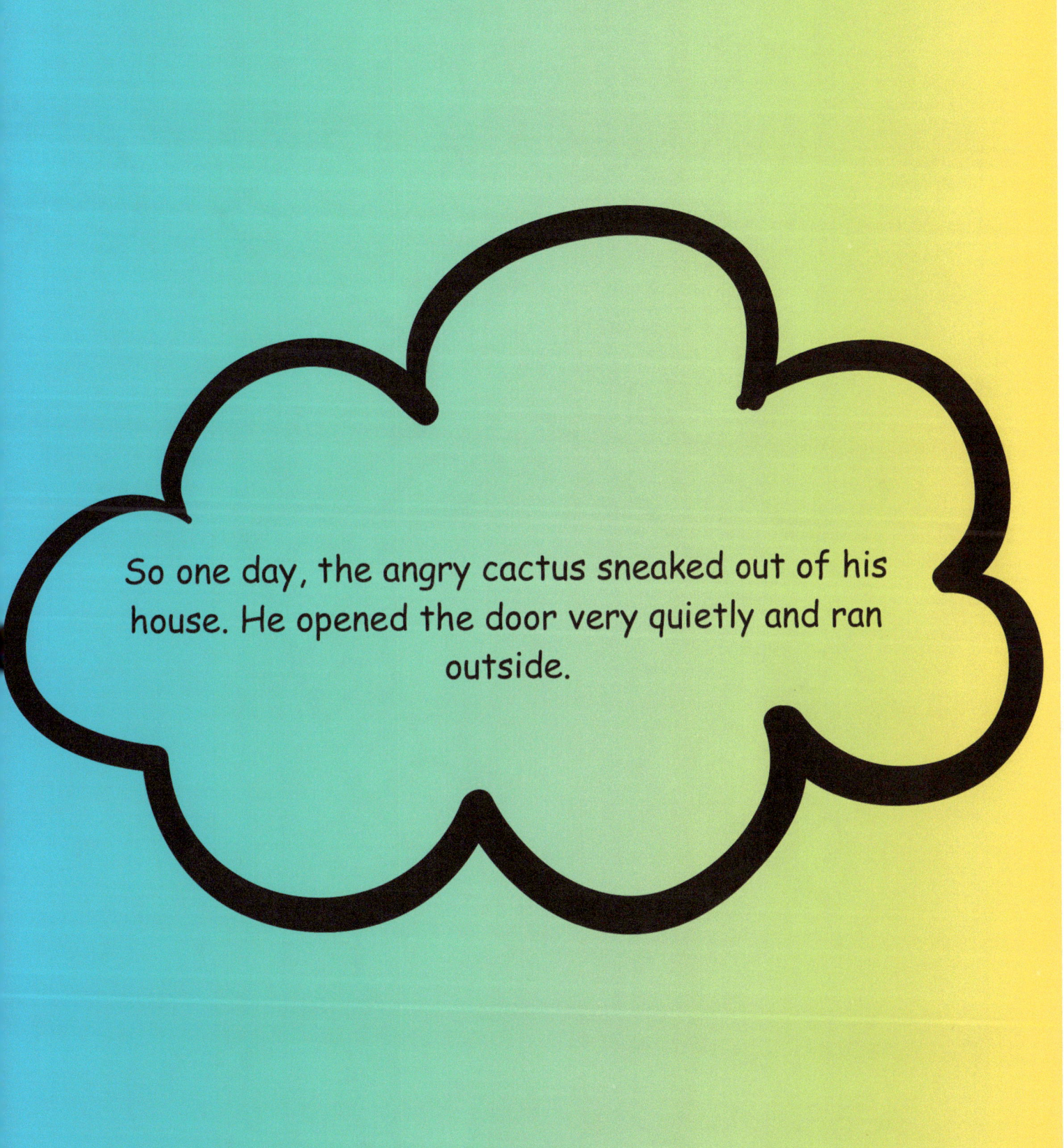

So one day, the angry cactus sneaked out of his house. He opened the door very quietly and ran outside.

While he started running, he stumbled across a big bad mummy. The mummy wanted to catch him, put him in his car and drive far away.

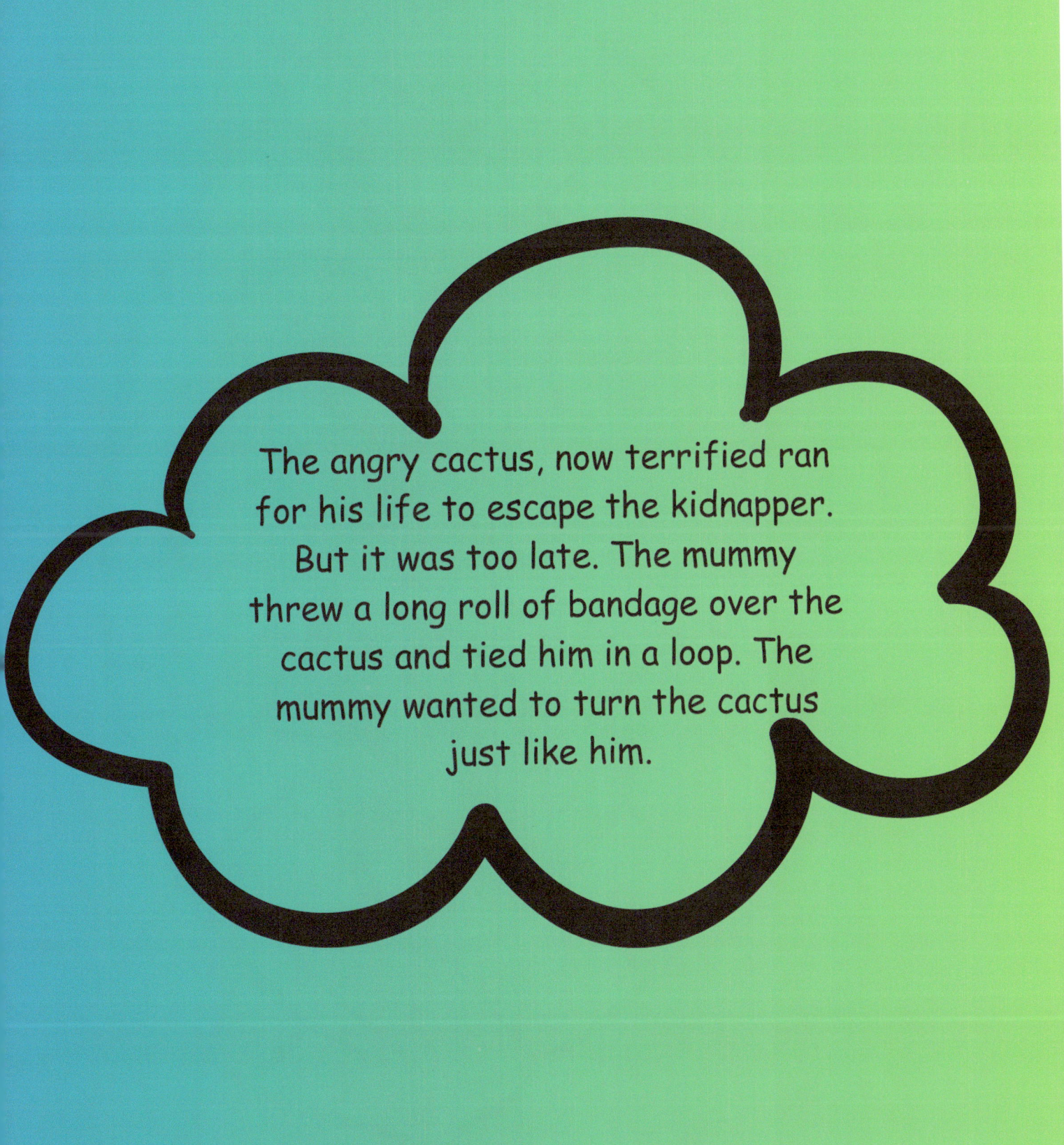

The angry cactus, now terrified ran for his life to escape the kidnapper. But it was too late. The mummy threw a long roll of bandage over the cactus and tied him in a loop. The mummy wanted to turn the cactus just like him.

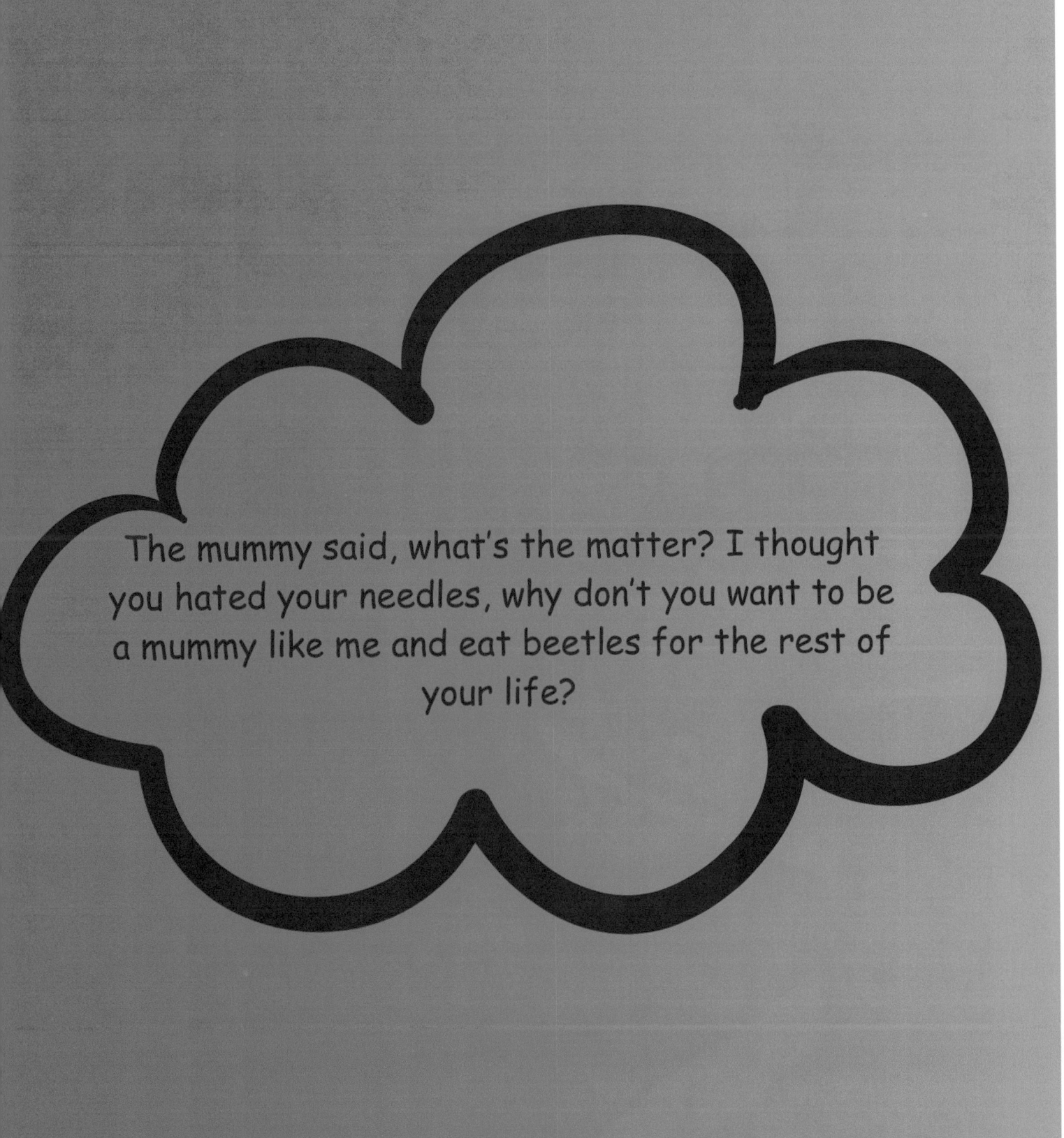

The mummy said, what's the matter? I thought you hated your needles, why don't you want to be a mummy like me and eat beetles for the rest of your life?

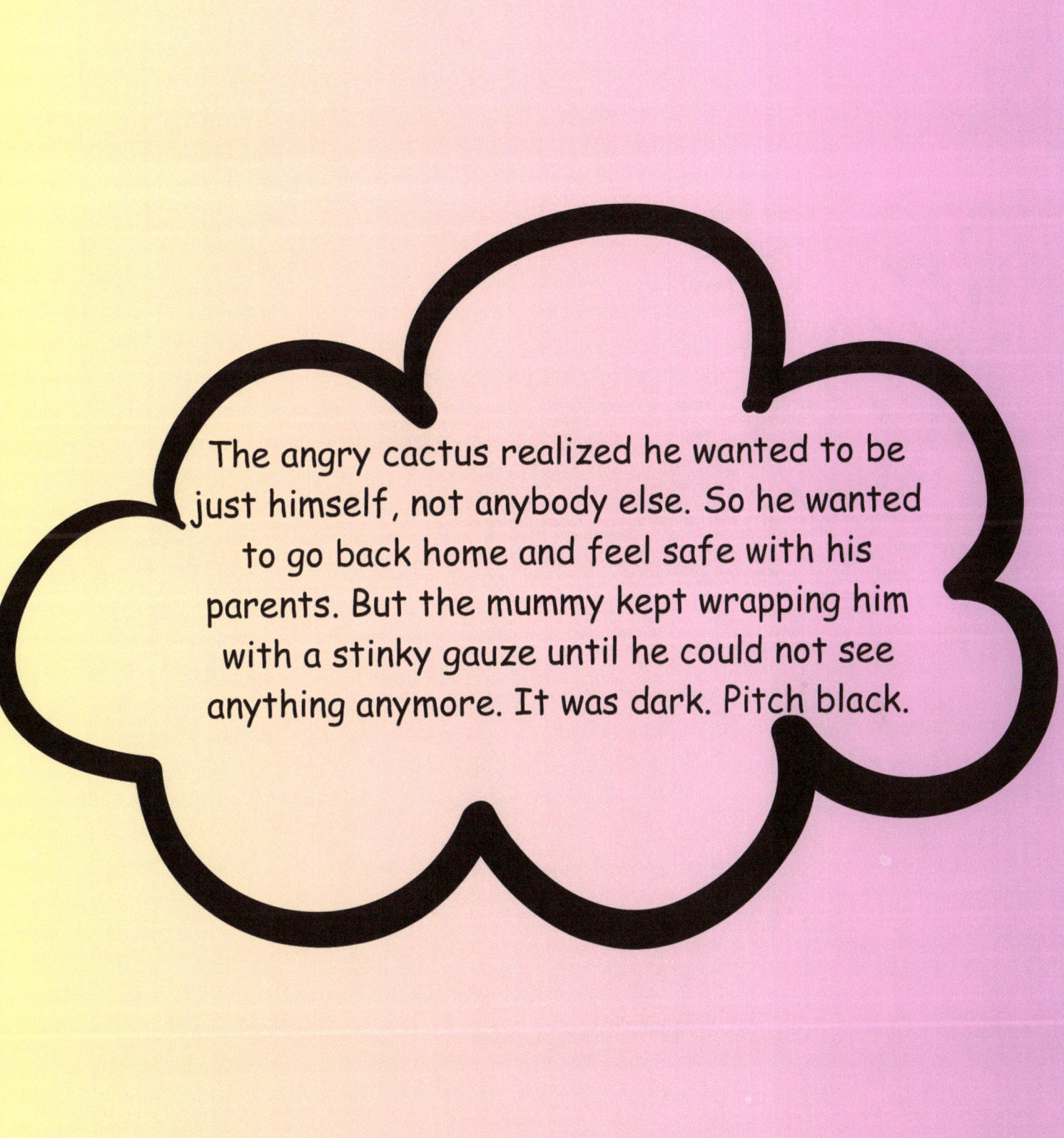

The angry cactus realized he wanted to be just himself, not anybody else. So he wanted to go back home and feel safe with his parents. But the mummy kept wrapping him with a stinky gauze until he could not see anything anymore. It was dark. Pitch black.

He started screaming and suddenly it felt like he was falling deep down.

He woke up. It was all a dream! He never left the house and there was never a bad mummy trying to kidnap him.

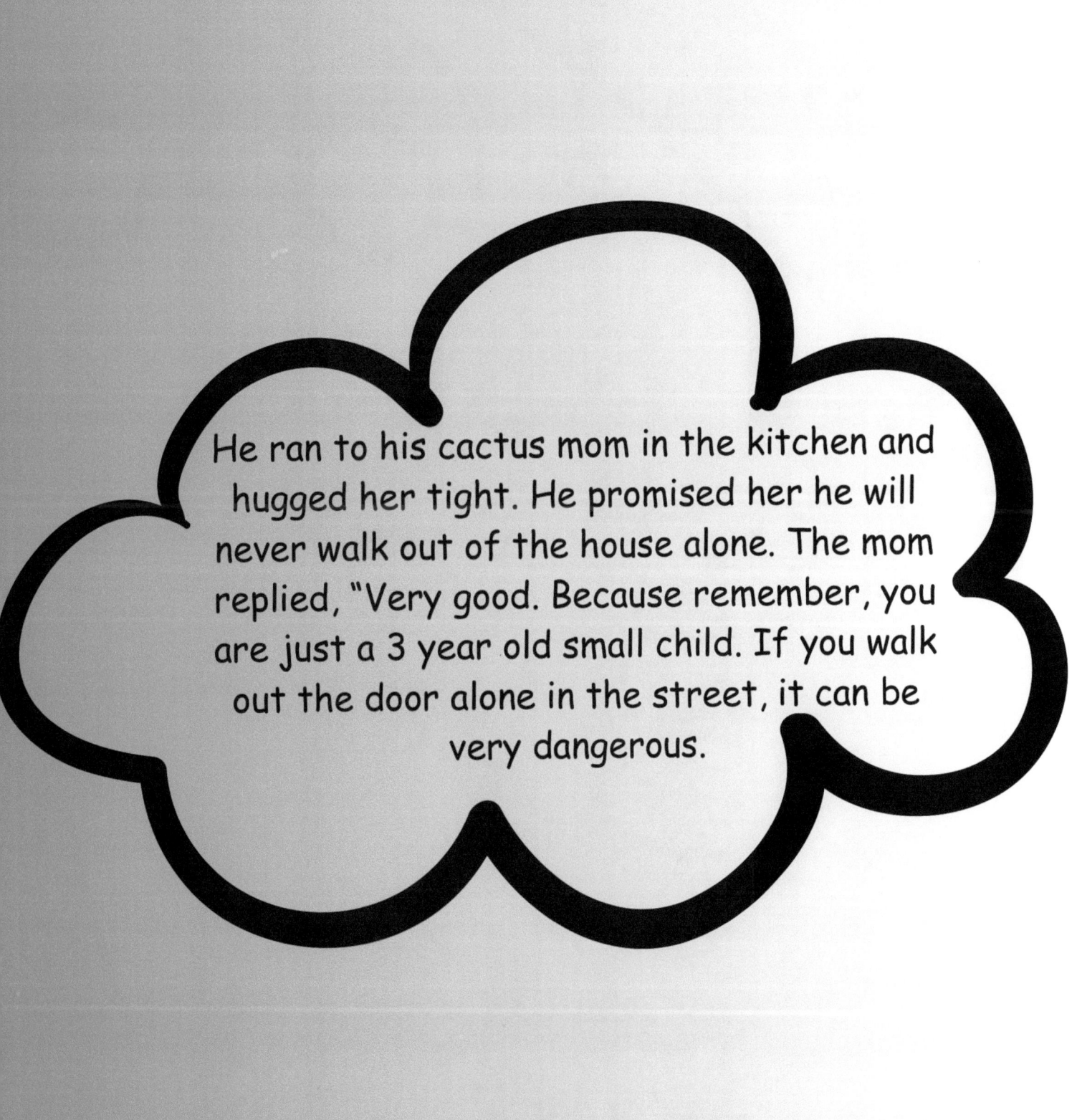

He ran to his cactus mom in the kitchen and hugged her tight. He promised her he will never walk out of the house alone. The mom replied, "Very good. Because remember, you are just a 3 year old small child. If you walk out the door alone in the street, it can be very dangerous.

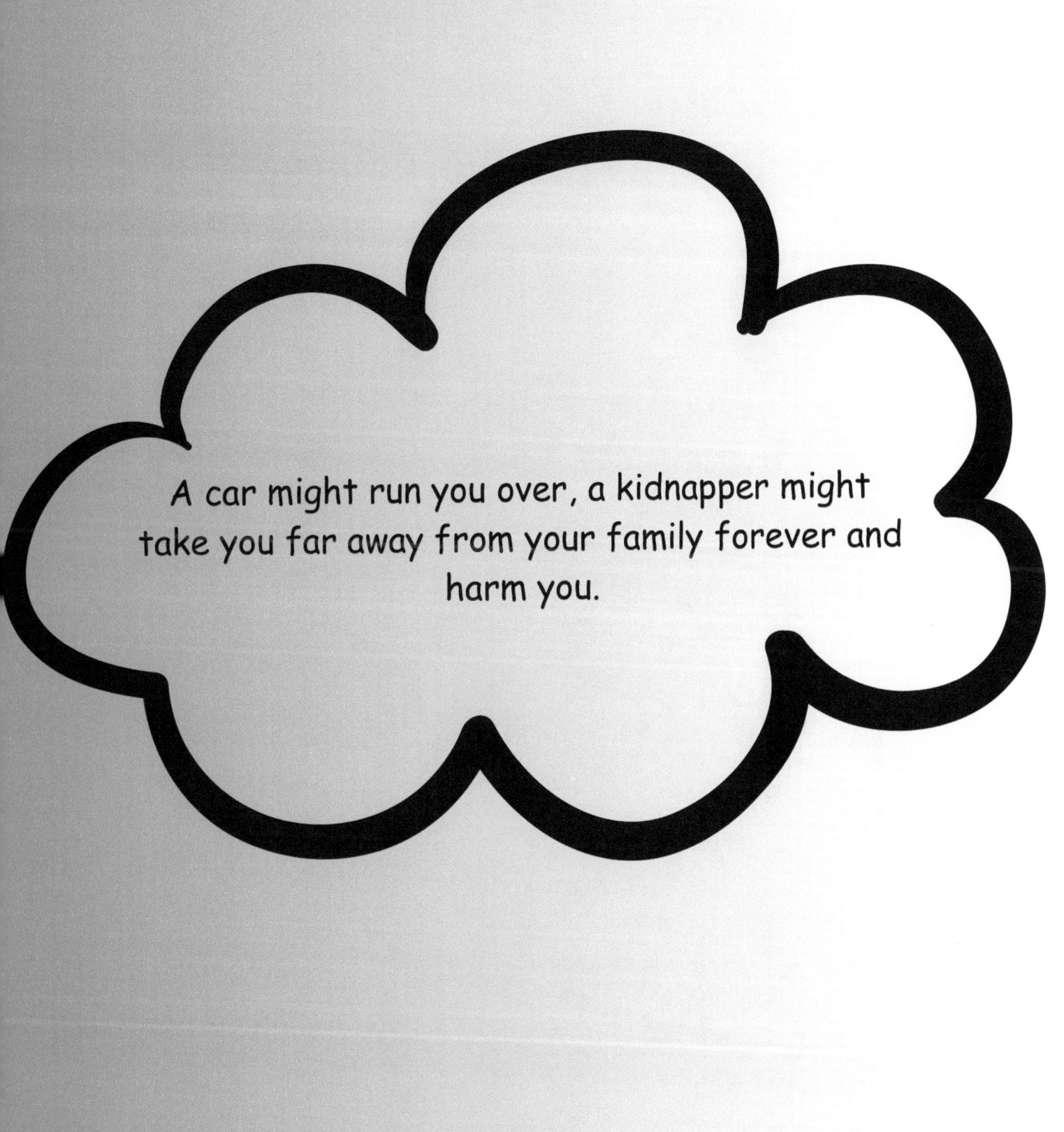

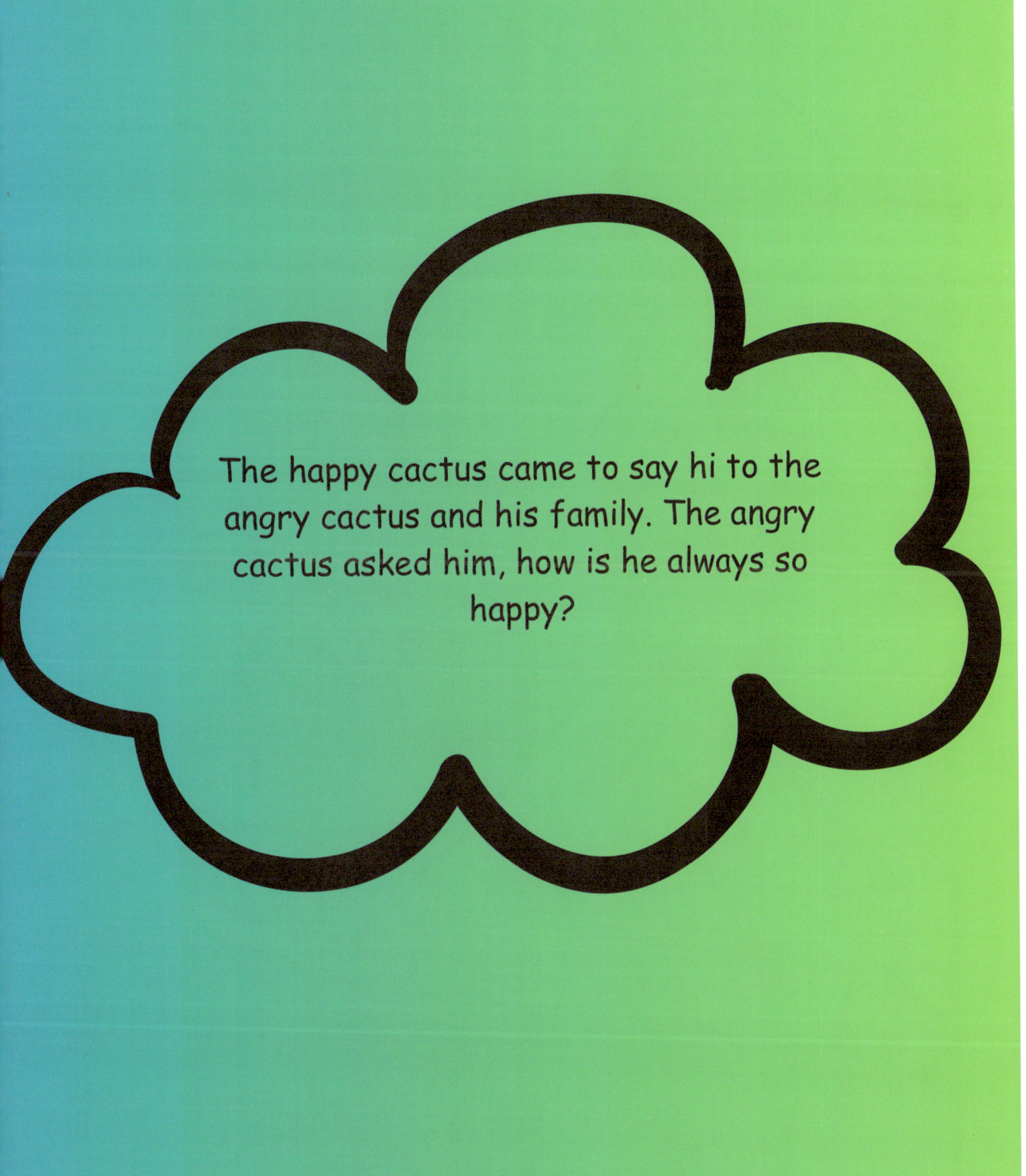

The happy cactus came to say hi to the angry cactus and his family. The angry cactus asked him, how is he always so happy?

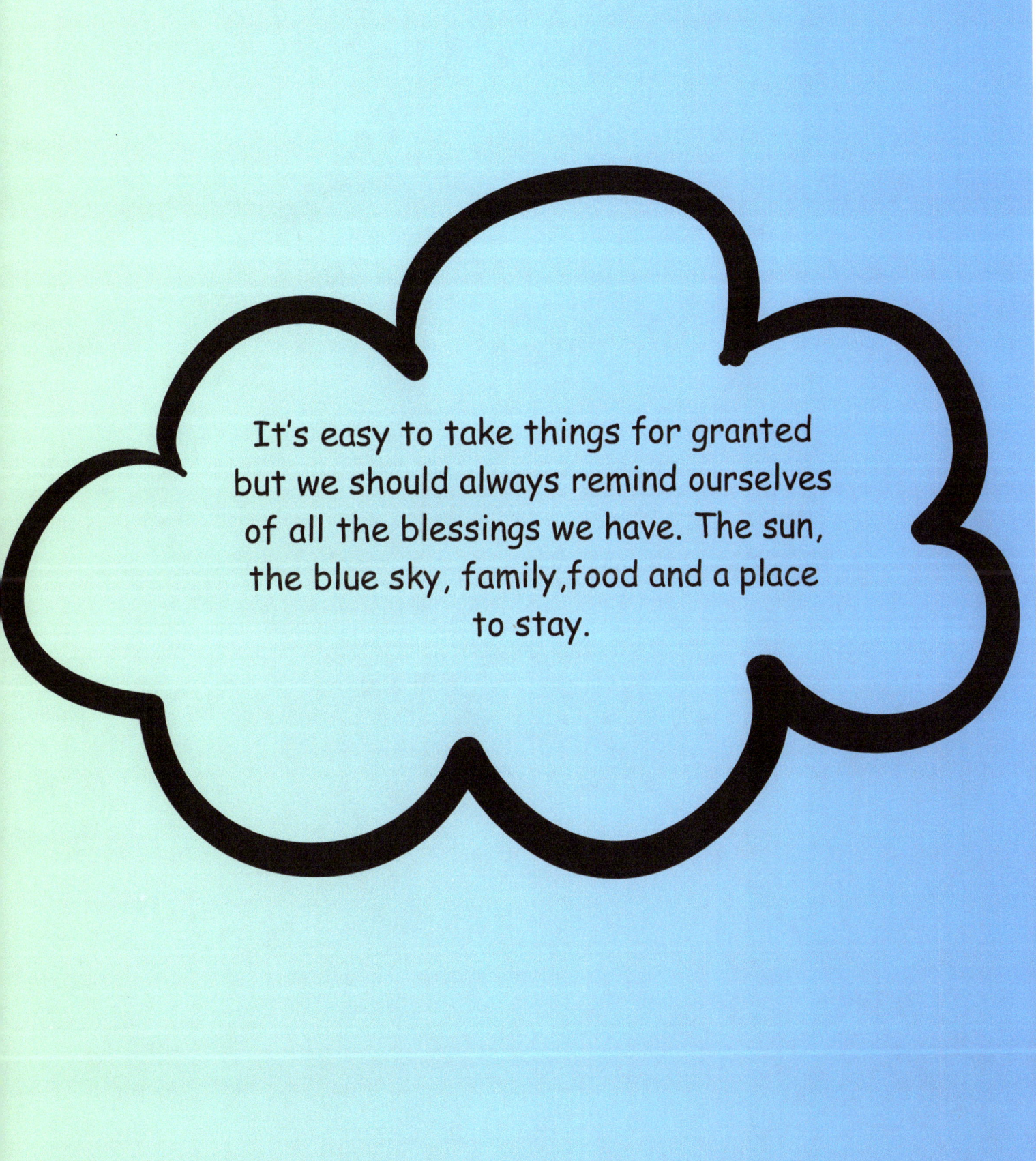

It's easy to take things for granted but we should always remind ourselves of all the blessings we have. The sun, the blue sky, family,food and a place to stay.

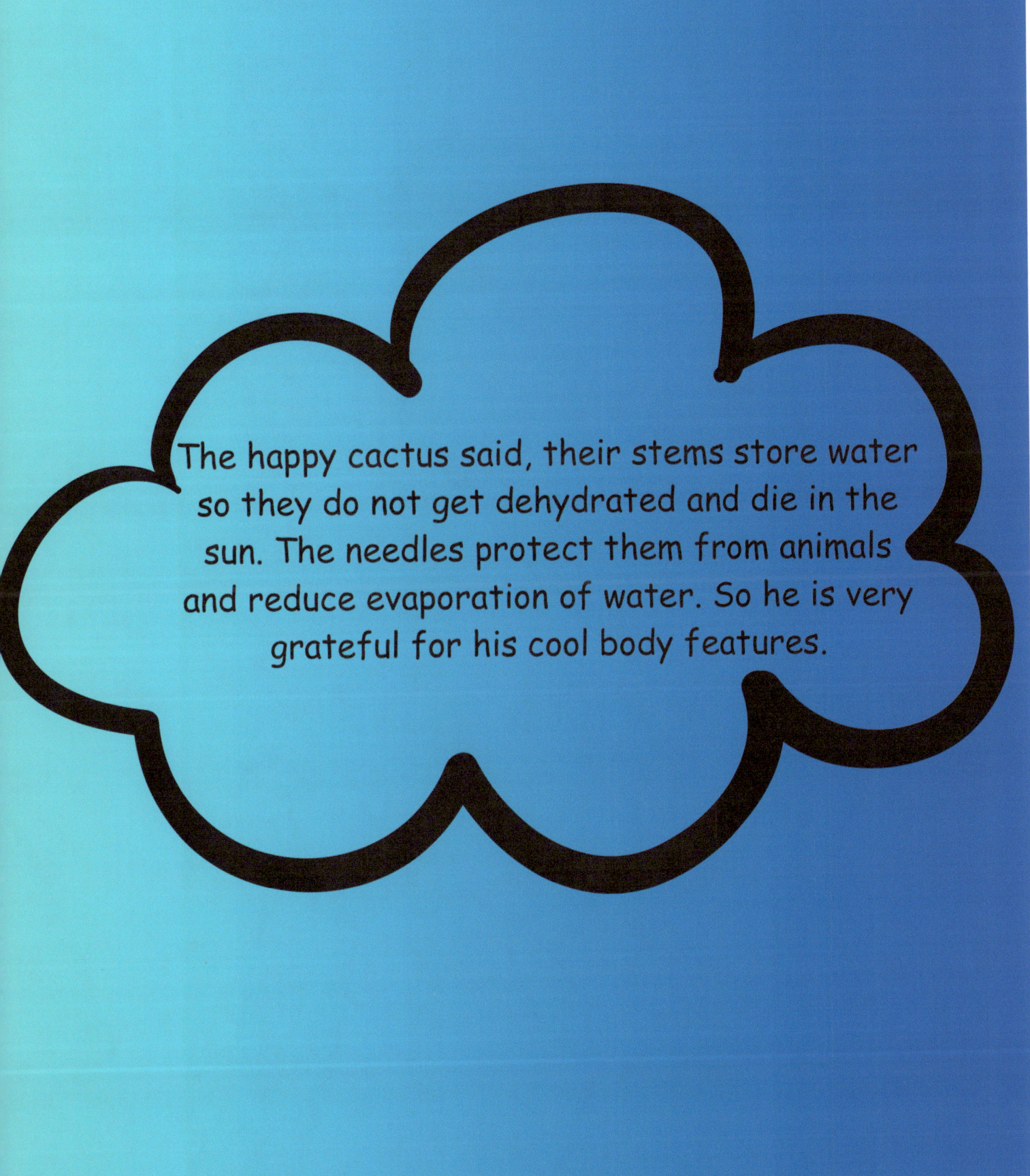

The happy cactus said, their stems store water so they do not get dehydrated and die in the sun. The needles protect them from animals and reduce evaporation of water. So he is very grateful for his cool body features.

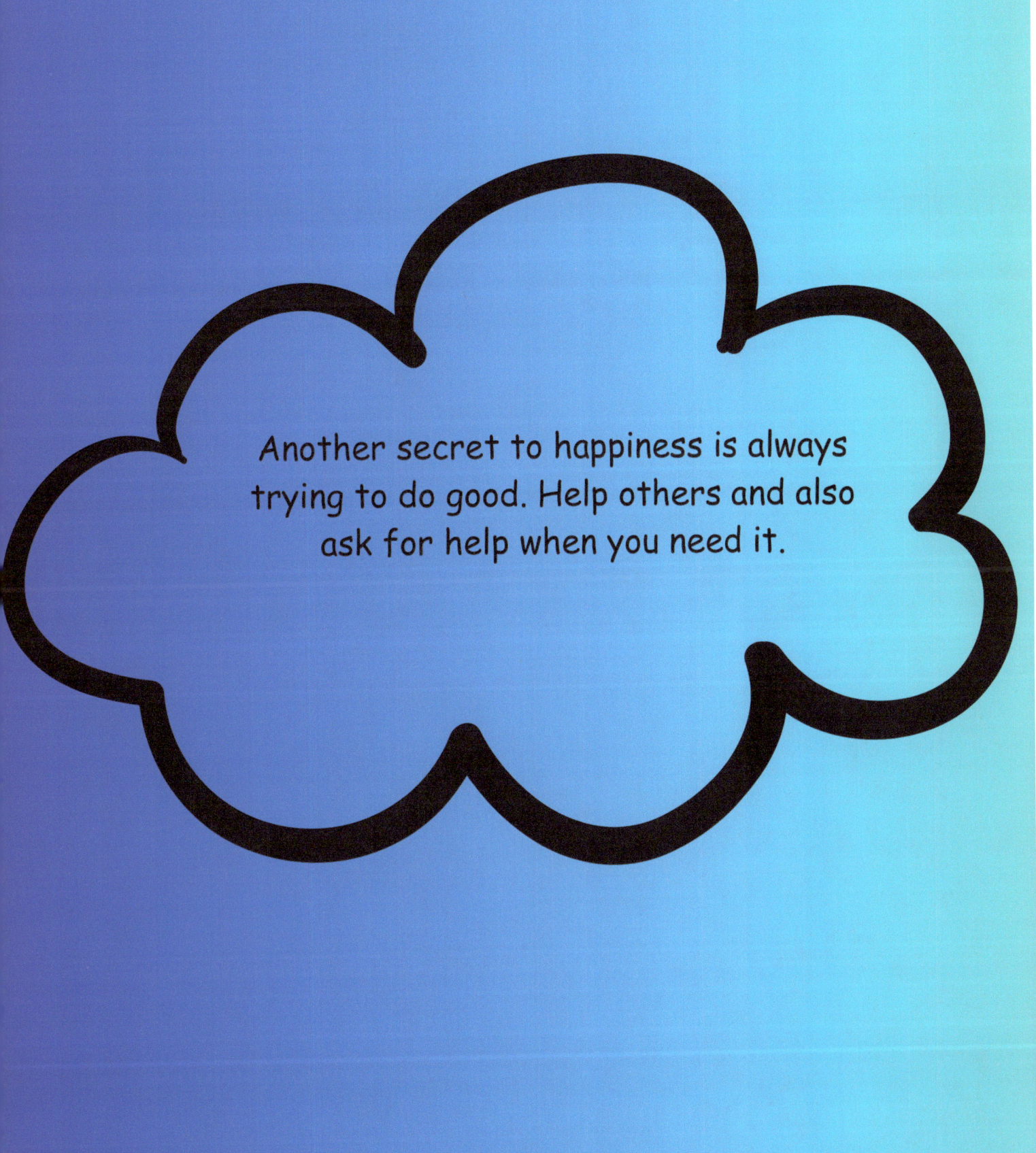

Another secret to happiness is always trying to do good. Help others and also ask for help when you need it.

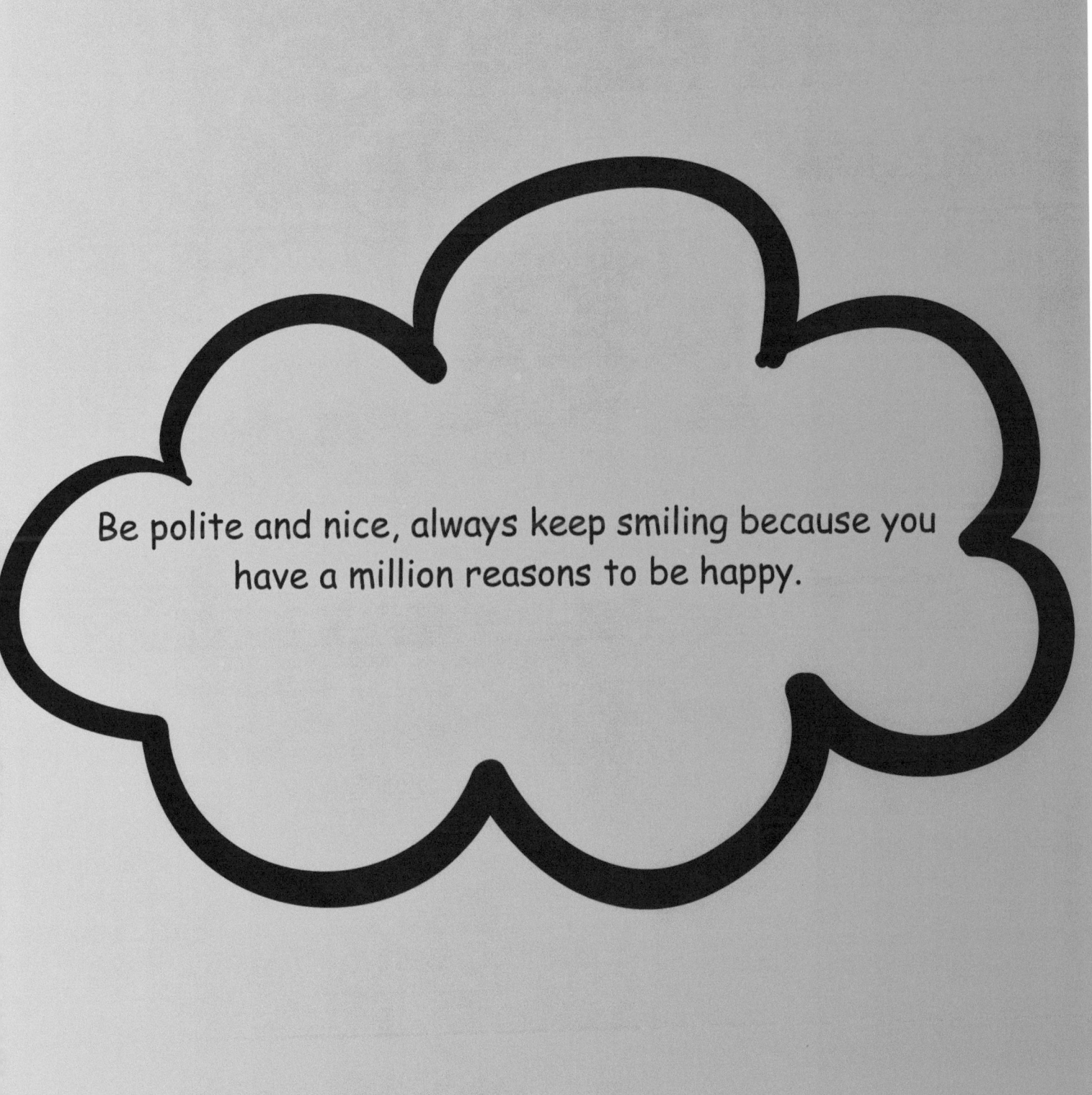

Be polite and nice, always keep smiling because you have a million reasons to be happy.

Always keep a healthy distance from toxic family members. As for friends, you can completely boycott them. Protect your own peace and do what it takes to keep your family safe.

You don't have to be liked by everyone, just the people who matters to you.